THE END OF NATURE

BOOKS OF POETRY BY CHAD WALSH

The End of Nature (1968)
The Unknowing Dance (1964)
The Psalm of Christ (1964)
Eden Two-Way (1954)
The Factual Dark (1949)

THE END OF NATURE

Poems by CHAD WALSH

FIRST EDITION

Published by

The Swallow Press, Inc.
1139 South Wabash Avenue
Chicago, Illinois 60605

LIBRARY OF CONGRESS CATALOG CARD NO. 72-75732

for Eva
my wife

Be dark with me and do not grieve
When the last mountains lose the day.
The lilacs of the law of love

Still blossom in our secret grove.
We planted roots deep as a vow.
Be dark with me and do not grieve.

In the light breeze their blossoms weave
Above our heads a private sky,
The lilacs of the law of love.

Above our heads the blossoms weave
A scented night the length of you.
Be dark with me and do not grieve.

They give us back the hearts we gave.
From planted earth the green hearts grow,
The lilacs of the law of love.

Beneath the hearts' roof, come and live
Beyond the twilight's afterglow.
Be dark with me and do not grieve
The lilacs of the law of love.

CONTENTS

1 *ODES*

Ode on a Plastic Stapes 3
Ode on the First Ape That Became a Man 4
Ode on a Student on LSD 6
Ode on the University of Mississippi 8

2 *ELEGIES*

Elegy for a Young Civil Rights Worker 15
In Memory of Sacco and Vanzetti: 1959 18
Elegy for Anyone 19
Elegy for President Kennedy 20

3 *QUINTINAS*

Bats at Dusk 27
The Archaic Hours 28
A Lullabye for Those Who Need it Most 29
Call it Alive 30
College President 31
A Quintina of Crosses 32

4 *CIRCULAR SONNETS*

Walking with a Young Grandson 35
Vermont Road 36
The Spacechild's Reverie 37
With These Plain Goods 38
The Stores of Night Have Sung My
Love Away 39

5 STORIES
Eyes 43
Noah At Ararat 45
Apollo's Song to Daphne 46
Dialogue at Dusk 48

6 SIGHTS
From an Inhabited Planet 55
Flight to Detroit 56
A Barn, a School, or a Church 57
White on White 58
The Chaos and Order of Snow 59
The Two Birches 60
Water Lilies 61
Darwin without Tears 62
Here in My Dry, Square Space 63
Puddle in the Road 64
Robins in the Spring 65
A Prayer to the Creatures and Their God 66

7 VARIETIES
Ropes of Nothing 69
Crypto-Jew 70
Homeless Feet 72
A Sequence of Saviours 73
Prayer to the Hanged Man 74
Silver and Sleep 75

Going, Growing, God 76
The Dance in Time 77
Two Prayers for 11:00 A.M. Sunday 78
Letter of Bartolomeo Vanzetti to His
Sister, Luigia 79
Poverty 82
Uneconomic Determinism 83
Port Authority Terminal, 9:00 A.M.
Monday 84
Circuit Poet 85
Fall in Finland 86
Finnish Saturday 87
November Night in Finland 88
Finland in Winter 90
Nuhjala 91
Country Churchyard in Finland 93
A Birthday Letter 94
Kalpa 95
Dream 97
The Angle of the Sunlight 98
Special Relativity 99
The Halo 100
The End of Nature 101

Notes on the Poems 102
Acknowledgments 104

1
ODES

Ode on a Plastic Stapes

for Dr. Rufus C. Morrow, surgeon

What God hath joined together man has put
Asunder. The stapes of my middle ear
Rests in some surgical kitchen midden.
Good riddance to an otosclerotic pest.
And welcome to the vibrant plastic guest
That shivers at each noise to let me hear.

What would the theologians make of this?
The bone God gave me petered out and failed.
But God made people, too. One of them sawed
A dead bone off and put a new one in.
I hear now through a storebought plastic pin.
Where God's hand shook, his creature's skill availed.

Dig where they bury me and you will find
A skeleton of bone perfected in plastic.
Gleam down the buried years, synthetic bone,
Await the judgment of the Resurrection,
The shining glory or the sharp correction
When calendars and clocks read chiliastic.

Will my old stapes rise, expel my plastic?
Do I own or do I merely borrow?
God is no divorce court judge. What man
Hath joined together, he will not put asunder.
Praise God who made the man who wrought this wonder,
Praise God, give thanks tomorrow and tomorrow.

Ode on the First Ape That Became a Man

Across the cracked savanna, as the sun
Blazed on the highest leaves of scattered trees
He stumbled home, cradling the little rodent
Stiff and dead. His stomach raged in pain,
His thick lips dripped with hungry spit. At last
He saw the nest of stones and broken branches
Where he had left her. The sudden sun set.
The quickening darkness chilled his clutching hands.
And he was cold inside. He ran to feed her.

Lifting a broken branch he made a sound,
Not word or name, a squealing call and summons.
No noise of body answered. The air was colder.
Vaguely he saw her there, chin to knees.
He touched her cheek. His hand sent waves of chill
Up the hair spirals of his arm. Slowly
He dropped the stiffened rodent, seized and shook her.
Her head jerked back and forth, the dead teeth clicked.
He wailed a grunting moan, shook her again.

His hunger ate a path, stomach to mouth.
The rodent lay, fat fleshed, close at his feet.
The hairy hand reached down, drew back, and hovered,
Then rose and masked the seeing of his eyes.
In double darkness he stood there while a life
Of pictures—if there were words they would be thoughts—
There were no thoughts but colors, sounds, and smells—
Tumbled disordered from that primal chaos
Where the bright trophies of two lives were housed.

There was a little cave half up a cliff,
Where they had hidden when the lions raged.
And there, by no decree of herd or custom,
And for no reasons he had images for,
He carried her, and laid her on the ground.
Then one by one he lifted rounded stones
From the dwindled stream and piled them up until
The opening was closed. Some cracks remained.
He gathered mud and filled them one by one.

Then in the darkness of the double night,
He shambled to his nest. The rodent lay there,
Fat and smelling of blood. A hungry stomach
Roared desires. He reached to take and eat.
But before his teeth could rip, he sprang outside,
In an innerness of uncouth images,
Carried the rodent to the cave. He took a stick
And made a hole. He pushed the rodent through.
He sealed the hole with mud. He limped home hungry.

In the double darkness of his nest,
He listened to the sounds of night. The roaring
Of lions, the whir of flying things, the wind
Dry and rough across the tattered grass.
A night bird's song came once, came twice to him,
Two tonic notes, the third a fifth above—
It sounded like Lo-nu-ha. She had been
A singing night. She had a name. "Lo-nu-ha,"
He wailed. In the word was the beginning.

Ode on a Student on LSD

I have my Bible, you have yours—
Huxley's Baedeker to magic doors,
And Alan Watts on cosmic joy.
I have my sacrament, the bread
And wine—good as His flesh and blood—
You have the little sugar cube
To grow you wings into the sky.

But that's a Christian metaphor.
You do not fly. You sit. And door
On door opens to let you see—
A technicolor cigarette flame;
An orange singing a holy name;
Beethoven's beatific rose.
You conjugate the verb *to be*.

I see you sitting by the wall,
A Buddha smile, "Nothing is all."
Your lids half closed with weight of knowing,
You smile at me in calm compassion.
I feel all nerves, desire, and passion.
You know it and I know your pity.
I wonder where we both are going.

You are not going, you are gone.
I'm not as easily turned on.
I pray, sometimes, or do a Quaker
Stint of silence, sometimes a breathless
But quickly dying hint of peace
Lingers briefly, but no worldshaker

Of a road-to-Damascus vision
To dazzle me to a blind decision.
And when I kneel along the rail
Beside my colleague's grown-up daughter
I think of how he loves Goldwater,
I scan her torso's silhouette,
And once again I fail, I fail.

You live by a brand of chemical grace,
I linger, last of a famous race,
The Puritans. You've heard about us.
We punch the time clocks, serve on committees,
Plan, but not build, heavenly cities,
Invent new pharmaceuticals.
You couldn't do without us.

You are the be-er, I the planner,
Miltown for me, for you nirvana.
Your eyes are closed and none can enter.
I hold the keys of *A* to *F*,
But you are blind and you are deaf
To solemn warnings from the dean
In the bright soul's secret center.

I'll leave you there (I must) and I'll
Resume my lecture notes on style,
And try to close my eyes for now
To the lecture of your private smile.

Ode on the University of Mississippi

September 30-31, 1962

1

As peacefully as Agincourt and Waterloo
The campus drowses in the mild gold day.
The rolling fields of Gettysburg ascend
Up from the Rebel soldier's granite feet
(Here the new Pickett led his final charge)
To the Lyceum where the marshals met
Snopes and Sartoris with tear gas; the Boston voice,
Pleading peace, is doubly stilled.

Time that takes into the scrapbook of old mementos
The exquisite inflections of a woman's muscles
Has sung September's night into time's story.
The Miss Americas, scented softly
As spring's first flowers,
In a loveliness of pastel frocks
Smile at the Lyceum on the way to class
Beneath the trees where maddened snipers perched
And fired with equal aim on besiegers and besieged.

Along the curved road of the burning faculty cars
The wraith of a memory of tear gas tingles
The nose of history.

2

From the scrub pine of the soul's hinterland
They came, from Alabama with shotguns on their knees,
By jet from Los Angeles.
Far from the Lyceum, in Baxter Hall,

The Negro said good night to his twenty-four marshals,
Read the newspaper, went to bed,
And slept to the programmed music of
          bottles hurtling down the hall.

Hotty, toddy, God A'mighty,
Who in the hell are we?
Flim flam, bim bam,
Ole Miss, by damn.

Never, Never, Never, Never, No-o-o Never Never Never,
We will not yield an inch of any field,
Fix us another toddy, ain't yieldin' to nobody,
Ross's standin' like Gibraltar, he shall never falter,
Ask us what we say, it's to hell with Bobby K,
Never shall our emblem go from Colonel Reb to Old Black Joe.

Hank, you marshal son of a bitch,
Your wife is home with a Nigger,
Nigger got a chigger,
Nigger got a chigger,
Two, one, four, three,
We hate Kennedy,
Nigger lover,
Nigger lover,
Your wife's got a Nigger
Under the cover,
I got a finger on the trigger,
We want Meredith,
We want Meredith,
We want Meredith,
Rope,
Rope,
Rope.

3

It ended.
When the last Sartoris retired to his dormitory,
And the ultimate Snopes had looked at the arriving soldiers
And thought better;
When the final volley of coke bottles had been thrown
Around Jefferson's courthouse square, close to the granite feet
Of the second Confederate veteran,
Bayonets flashed,
The men with gasoline cans for the Negro churches
Ran or put their hands up.
Like all things, it ended, as things end.

4

Observe (for science's sake) a virtuous wife,
Mated in bed; observe a well-trained whore;
Measure their motions and the medical data—
Heart beat, pulse, blood pressure, temperature—
And say, studying the graphic zigs and zags,
Which body moved in love, and which for hire.
But science is too simple. Who can say (the charts
Omit this item) when and whether gain
Is teased to lust, and lust is coaxed to love,
Singing old songs of movies from the fifties,
Stirring remembrances of a TV serial,
Rocking in sweet time with the reflex muscles,
Until pure love is immaculately born,
Briefly, at the baptism of orgasm.

So those who fought with bricks and chunks of concrete,
Iron rods for spears, bottles of looted acid,
Rifles and shotguns, Molotov cocktails,
Saw before them the gray tanks of Budapest,
The helmets of foreign mercenaries,

The snarls of the secret police writing down names.
The orgasm of hate gave plenary indulgence
For venial sins and sealed them freedom fighters.

5

The circling seasons come again,
Snow and harvest, drought and rain,
Flower and leaf and naked tree,
Leaf and bud and circling bee,
Death and life and love and hate,
Freedom free to choose its fate,
Nothing new under the sun,
A battle won and lost and won,
And won and lost, Gettysburg, Pickett—

Northern stranger, in your thicket
Of hates and hopes and private lies,
Where nothing nasty ever dies;
In the white suburban tracts,
Spared the madder public acts;
Where a dream of innocence
Drives you out of common sense
To apocalyptic visions
And a madman's sane decisions,
Behold your dark heart magnified
Upon this southern screen.
Something northern also died.
Death comes, death goes. Keep your bayonet clean.

2
ELEGIES

Elegy for a Young Civil Rights Worker

He met his name in the double heart of darkness—
The South, his soul. Like a despised necktie
From a suburban birthday he sloughed his meekness.

He had been here before, and he had not,
Where black was white, white black, and the bright heart
Rode the red breakers of the summer's heat.

The phallic bus parted the womb of the South
And the soft shabbiness invited deeper
Straight to the spasm of organic truth.

Magnolia blossoms, sweet as a funeral parlor,
Courthouses where the brutal sheriffs lurked,
Plantations, columns of a sinister pallor,

Signs of "colored" and "white," a deepening blur
Of Faulkner faces—Snopes, Sartoris, Christmas—
Fearful laughter. He had been here before.

At a rest stop, his father's gray eyes scowled
From the pump boy's glance. Hate flashed at hate.
Back to the bus. In the new night he rolled

Nearer the soul's secret, down the straight lane
Of a freeway as virginal and spare
As an IBM card. He dreamed of rain.

In the gray morning, faces black and white
Blazed by at sixty miles. And white was black
And black was white at the heart's judgment seat.

The bus arrived, and in a bleeding flush
Of dawn, into a terror of slurred voices,
He stepped down, stiffened in the mortal flesh.

From Dostoevski surged a coal black face
Gleaming with the dark fathom of the holy
And led him silent to a trysting place.

The parking lot, the car, he squeezed inside
Into a flash of faces white and black,
By the risen sun toned with the gold of blood.

Through streets as devious as a trial's stages,
Perfumed by gross shrubs redolent of sheets,
From the mid time back to prior ages

Of soul he traveled and the horror of pulse
Beat fast behind his modesty of skin
Beside the black cheeks of his mother's face.

A white frame church, the only one he'd entered
Since God had died in the tenth grade, enclosed him
In a preverbal warmth. And he was hunted

By intimations of organic truth,
By faces white as a cemetery's trove,
Black as the first gravedigger's spade of wrath.

They broke the sandwiches and ate. They drank
The coffee of an integral communion.
Someone stood up and prayed. He tried to think.

A surge of singing purged his cluttered mind.
Outside they formed the ritual procession.
He marched. He held a blackly human hand.

From sidewalks glared the troopers one by one,
From opened doors and windows snarled the red faces
Of every hate his emptied heart had known.

His lips were singing, "We shall overcome,"
His ears received the promise back in chorus,
The Atman's monotone said, "Om Om Om."

And all was well. When the gray eyes of rage
Sprang forward, dual suns of blazing doom,
And time retreated to a knee-high age,

When the red face lunged, and a black club
Whirled white against the purifying sun
It met the meekness of his proffered skull.

Nothing was black or white. In a brief prism
Of every heightened blaze of mescaline
His soul erupted from the bony prison;

His father laid the club aside and smiled,
And led his mother off to a secret bed,
And every perishing color blessed and failed.

In Memory of Sacco and Vanzetti: 1959

To walk down the street now, to see the Common
In its accustomed desultory life,
One would almost say no ration of voltage
Could matter very much, nor Boston ever cease.

The still pure white of magnolias, flecked
With red, sweetens the cloying air.
The subway digests and disgorges. There is love,
Still fumbling love, one supposes, somewhere.

Up the hill the gilded statehouse stands,
Costlier than a sepulcher. The shabby years
Move in. If you had second sight
You would see the uncut grass, the cracked arches.

The sailors on Scollay Square hunt whores
With dutiful diligence. Sex
Is a kind of penance. The joy of the nerves
Is dulled in the dying city.

The spring sky is close, a low haze,
As it was one August. Magnolia blossoms
Drip their dried blood. The slow zombies
Cross the Common, recross, with fixed eyes.
Jerusalem, Jerusalem.

Elegy for Anyone

The machine performed its public motions
Under sealed orders. Lungs filled and flattened,
The heart gave pressure to blood.
Obscure workshops produced their quota
Of hormones, according to the tested formulas.
The mind idled on perelandran seas
And fretted for deeper oceans.

The machine stopped by discrete instalments.
Blood settled in gravity, nails and hair
Continued a micron of growth,
And slowly with the finality of geological change
The ecology of cells endured
The anarchy of irreversible chemistry.

The great billows lifted him lightly
And he weighed no more than God.

Elegy for President Kennedy

November 22, 1963

1

Say that the Dallas madness touched a speck
Of kindred mind.
Infection found its culture, rose like yeast.
The seeing eyes stared blind,
The well-tempered brain slept, a final wreck.
And Dallas swelled into a bloated beast
Whose tail
Noosed tight around our local galaxy
And lashed Andromeda. Wail,
Ye daughters of the dawn. Out of the east
Rode life. The king is dead. And see
The darkness close the west.

Among such books as Texan children read,
Almost nothing crouched and watched
Through the thin lines that drew a perfect cross,
Till at the center where they met and touched
The point transfixed a head.
He saw the crumpled brown hair toss
In glints of gold,
The god of sunlight and the bright moon his queen.
His finger twitched. The air turned cold,
The earth was cold before the triple underpass.
His finger twitched again, again.
He looked a last time, smiled, and left his kneeling place.

2

O weep for Adonais, he is dead.

At the entrance of the north gate of the house of the Lord,
Behold, there sat women weeping for Tammuz.
The wailing is for the shrunken ears of barley.
The wailing is for the dry bed of the great river.
The wailing is for the wedded ones and withered love.
The wailing is for the perishing children and their
forsaken toys.

O weep for Adonais, he is dead.

Deep in the Land of Silence
Wakeful Osiris sleeps.
The dwelling of the inhabitants of the west
Is dark forever.
The east of the sun never enters.
The north of the wind never freshens the heart.
They have taken the guardian away to the dark house
of the west.

O weep for Adonais, he is dead.

The tamarisk in the garden has drunk no water.
The olive in the field has brought forth no fruit.
The willow lies prone, its great roots crack in the sun.
The herb in the garden has drunk no water.
The split pomegranate bares its bleeding seeds.

When will the anemone bloom red in Arlington?

Ye daughters of the dawn,
Bright in the eastern sun,
Wail, wail,
Rend your garments, wrench your locks.
The god is dead. The dark earth speaks.
Dead, dead.
Wail, wail
Till the anemone blooms red
And the sun blesses the risen god
With gold caresses on his golden head.

3

The surly seasons grunt and creak
And move along the yearly track.
The dirty snows of winter fall,
The shoddy buds of April swell,
The leaves of May are garish green,
November comes, another one,
The dirty snows, the sinking nights,
The caged gorilla breeds and eats,
And stocks are bought and stocks are sold,
Soldiers are drilled, soldiers are killed,
And spaceprobes photograph the moon.
In Arlington the grass is green.
All flowers blossoms now save one,
The red anemone.

4

It is all a manner of speaking.
Myth is myth, history is death. The finger that tensed
With the weight of megatons is lax with the stiffness
Of a short pencil of steel to the brain.

On tape recordings the Boston voice
(Something of Ireland still, not wholly Harvard)
Still speaks, in old video tapes the admonishing finger jabs.
So in marble, Caesar survived his Brutus, so Lincoln in a
Brady photograph,
So in the memory of a deposed Khrushchev your Cuban
face yet lives.
You are dead.
For a moment, an hour, we made meaning,
Prepared in the heart the righteous slaughter of the Texans,
The Birchers, the haters who had felled you. Burn and kill,
burn and kill,
The heart sang its blood song above the hasty coffin of the
New Lincoln.
The cold smile of a demented Marxist said only, "I am!
I am! I am!"

(O weep for Adonais. He is dead.)

The only meaning is there is no meaning.

5

Good night, sweet prince, sleep sound.
The old earth dully makes its yearly round.

The old earth daily spins.
Day dies to night. Another day begins.

Brightness falls from the air.
The radios and politicians blare.

The sun is farther, colder.
The world is smaller, emptier, and older.

The poet's words are dry with age, and trite.
Sleep sound, sweet prince. Good night.

3
QUINTINAS

Bats at Dusk

Because each window has a screen
I like to sit on the porch, watch the bats
Skimming the lake, eating a passage through
The shoals of gnats, riding the broken
Back of the day and soaring

On sudden errands high above the screen
Of pines and birches lining the shore. A broken
Sunset gilds the height of their soaring
And for a space, heaven's small angels have ventured through
On the gliding wings of golden bats.

And when a slowly soaring
Crescent of moon comes climbing through
A nest of random clouds, I see the bats,
Baby pterodactyls, veering past the screen,
Wings tipped in silver. Nothing is broken

Except the bony frames of gnats, soaring
Too late and slow to flee the swift sortie of bats.
Looking through
The fine mesh of screen
I cannot see the little bodies broken.

Only by the twitching movements of bats
Do I mark the moment their small universe is broken
And death takes them soaring
Black as a stomach's secret, through
The silver of moon, past my window screen.

When will the screen be broken, bats come soaring through?

The Archaic Hours

We hear them call,
We see them gambol, stride and wait,
Those frozen centuries, the archaic hours
Of sleep, when the old gods and devils know
That they can come and go at will.

They hide in cluttered cellars during the Christian hours
And rarely call,
Or if they do, it's simple to say No
Or make a mock of deafness. They can wait,
Knowing the peaks and chasms of the will.

Sometimes they strike the poses of the Nō
In drama's ritual beyond the easy call
Of the heart's simple, sensate will
Or the gospel's grave and massive weight.
Their play is ours.

The other side of good and evil, they wait,
A Mardi Gras of serious masks, the call
To magic caves, the wind's monsters, the hours
When shamans seek the soul's double, and no
Plato or Moses reins the loosened will.

By the first hairy Adam's will
They are our legacy, on call
And calling us to where the first images wait
In the bright terror of their unbegotten beauty, the hours
That stiffly dance, the thrust lip intoning, "Know, know,
know."

Hours call, wait no will.

A Lullaby for Those Who Need it Most

Lumbering hulk of cellular poundage, sleep.
The trees that fed you sweet and bright are bare
Of fruit and leaf. There's nothing left to see—
Black skeleton, white snow, dun bushes—spare
Your gluttonous eye. Descend the darkness, meet

The ugly roots. There's time and time to spare,
Before you choose the posture of the sleep
You choose. Learn from the winter bear
Light breathing in the darkness where you meet
The cavern's staring eye that cannot see.

There's nothing here for the hungry belly's meat
Or hungrier soul. Time's pantry shelves are bare.
Dead soul, then be beginning to despair.
And in the sleep of dead things dream of sleep
And float deluded on a fragrance of sea.

Dream of an ocean goddess who will bear
A child. Be father and the son. And eat
In dreams a magic fruit to set you free
From the spell's task, and leap
Into the brightness of remembered air.

Sleep deeper now and cease to dream. Bare
Are the goddess' breasts but not for you. Prayer
Is the lowest finger of the deepest root,
The needle in the heart. Hush now and sleep,
Revolving dreamless, day, night. Lullaby.

Bare. Sleep spare. Meet. See.

Call it Alive

A little pond where cattle came to drink,
A grove of chestnut trees, alive
With white blossoms and fall's brown burred food,
Robins in the mud
Tugging the worm from the earth's guts.

All things were alive—
The stepping stones across the swamp of mud
Rose under my feet. And I would drink
At brooks that flowed to me coming. Food
Sang into my guts.

The cattle's food
Is the parch of grass. The robin's mud
Is stiff with drought. Blight guts
The chestnut grove. The brook that gave me drink
Is dead. I am alive.

I am alive?
The robin's bill shatters against the mud,
The tortured cattle low for drink.
Another hunger eats my guts.
I have no chestnut burs to crack for food.

O ruined pond, alive
With scum from the edges. When will the brook flow drink
To me and the other beasts, and flood the mud
Into a robin's wealth of worms? Where's food
(The chestnuts bloom no more) for the eye's guts?

Drink dry mud for the gut's food. Call it alive.

College President

They made him president. On each committee
He was ex officio. He held the power
Of Yes, No, and Maybe in his office.
He dreamed at times of an absurd purity
Of soul, a paradise that he had lost.

The passions of all souls flowed to his office,
And like the buck they stopped there, lost
Among the filing cabinets, where committee
Reports lay sleeping. When he spoke, the power
Of principalities dimmed his purity

Of vision (P. R., trustees). Lost
In memories of his departed purity
When he had held the chalk, and a committee
Was nothing but a faculty joke, the power
Of fancy could metamorphose his office

Into a classroom, where the pristine purity
Of truth and beauty eddied; when his office
Was the log and he Mark Hopkins. At a committee
Meeting among the friends that he had lost,
Sometimes he almost auctioned off his power

To any bidder, and almost said, "The lost
Sheep bleats for pity; into the purity
Of your daily gripes receive me back!" But office
Phone calls always claimed him in time, the power
Of the accustomed day, the next committee,

The day ahead, a new committee, the power
Of Yea and Nay, the lost purity
Filed under *P* somewhere in the office.

A Quintina of Crosses

Beyond, beneath, within, wherever blood,
If there were blood, flows with the pulse of love,
Where God's circle and all orbits cross,
Through the black space of death to baby life
Came God, planting the secret genes of God.

By the permission of a maiden's love,
Love came upon the seeds of words, broke blood,
And howled into the Palestine of life,
A baby roiled by memories of God.
Sometimes he smiled, sometimes the child was cross.

Often at night he dreamed a dream of God
And was the dream he dreamed. Often across
The lily fields he raged and lived their life,
And heaven's poison festered in his blood,
Loosing the passion of unthinkable love.

But mostly, though, he lived a prentice's life
Until a singing in the surge of blood,
Making a chorus of the genes of God,
Flailed him into the tempest of a love
That lashed the North Star and the Southern Cross.

His neighbors smelled an alien in his blood,
A secret enemy and double life;
He was a mutant or an obscene cross
Outraging decency with naked love.
He stripped the last rags from a proper God.

The life of God must blood this cross for love.

4
CIRCULAR SONNETS

Walking with a Young Grandson

When Marcus runs I give a leap
And lift him with a swoop and sweep.
He makes a sound that sounds like "beep."

I walk him where the woods are dark,
I show him where the bullfrogs live,
And how the lilies go to sleep.

Sometimes he's very positive;
I want to trot, he wants to creep,
I want to coo, he wants to bark.

He hands me shiny stones to keep.
Our homeward path is a laggard arc.
My heart is punctured as a sieve.

I have the good of seven sons
When Marc meanders, skips, or runs.

Vermont Road

When I walked down the road today
The goldenrod was thick as hay.
Autumn is surely on the way.

When I walked down the country road
The purple asters swayed and glowed.
In maple trees the first red showed.

Along the gravel road walked I
Beneath the woven blue of sky
Straight down the season that must die.

Today I walked the long road down,
I walked the seven miles from town.
The sumac wore a crimson crown.

I walked the summer weeks away
When I walked down the road today.

The Spacechild's Reverie

I'll throw a dart into the sun.
I'll give the Martians quite a start.
This thing at least they never know—
The way to cut a star in two.

A very little dart will do.
Smaller the dart, bigger the fun.
I'll throw it now and watch it go
Ah slowly for the solar heart.

Sit here and see it fall apart.
Count from a trillion down to one.
It may explode before you're through
Especially if you are slow.

But it will make a pretty glow.
My dart into the sun I'll throw.

With These Plain Goods

The gift of hands is all I vow.
Then take them as my best for now.
With these plain goods I thee endow.

Perhaps your smooth skin understands
Shy fingers freed and set adrift
To rove the cartographic ball

And ride the great waves as they lift
And make the seas their banquet hall
And steer far out from gull-bright lands.

Perhaps your smooth skin understands.
I hear the blind-deep ocean call
And sunken rivers warm and swift.

The waves of you will teach me how,
And stroke by stroke I'll swim my vow.

The Stores of Night Have Sung My Love Away

The stores of night have sung my love away.
Where she has gone I cannot find the way.
Small crickets of the dark, sing Wellaway.

I tracked her on the lonely moors,
I couldn't see her little spoors.

I caught and sent a singing dove,
He flew me to an empty grove.

I ran to where a rainbow hung
And couldn't climb the second rung.

I ran beyond the speed of light,
I think she hid away in fright.

I asked the crickets at their play.
They hadn't anything to say.
The stores of night have sung my love away.

5
STORIES

Eyes

The face he saw in the pool
Was almost yours or mine,
Or at least your neighbor's face
On any subway line.

But there was his face in the water
Giving as good as he gave.
He had two sets of eyes
Which he hadn't seen in the cave.

But now as he watched the self
That watched him from the pool,
A third self smiled from somewhere,
The second grinned back like a fool,

And higher than cloud or sun
Two steady, invisible eyes
Surveyed the earth's three selves
Now dwindled to baby size.

They say he ran back to the cave,
And never saw eyes again,
But his sons went forth from the darkness
And cast their lot to be men.

One looked in the pool, and hastened
To cover the cave with art;
Another built an altar,
And plunged a knife in a heart.

The third was a harum-scarum
That eyes could never vex.
He bought himself a harem
And specialized in sex.

The fourth made money and kept it,
The fifth did good by the hour,
And both were too busy to see
The eyes that grin and glower.

The sixth invented *kōans*,
Discovered the buds of peyote,
Closed his own eyes and conjured
The eyes of a cosmic coyote,

And looked with the eyes that he saw
And was the eyes of his seeing,
Returned to the primal cave
And unitary being.

Noah at Ararat

"Raven, raven, what did you see? A leaf,
An olive tree? A blade of grass?"
"The blue sky overhead,
A pair of pretty zebras floating dead,
A round sea green as glass."

"Dove, dove, where did you set your dainty foot?
Where will you go to build a nest?"
"I looked and saw no tree,
I saw the waves and graves of the cold gray sea,
A pale sun in the west."

"Dove, dove, what have you brought to cheer my soul?
What have you found, my darling thief?"
"The dead men surged and floated,
I saw the dead men, blotched and splotched and bloated.
But I brought you an olive leaf."

"Dove, dove, where are you now, my faithful dove,
Why have you been so long away?
I see a blue of sky.
When will I see your white wings flying by?
Your mate will droop and die."

"Japheth and Ham and Shem, go call your mother,
And wake the birds and beasts and snakes,
Check on the mother sow,
Hitch up the mules and horses, sharpen the plow,
And file the hoes and rakes."

How big the world is. I had forgotten.
And bigger as the sea recedes.
"Hurry, it's getting dark."
And we were warm and snug inside the ark . . .
"And don't forget the seeds!"

Apollo's Song to Daphne

Why do you run so fast, so fast,
Daphne, why do you run?
Look back and see the fire of my face
And warm your heart in the sun.

Why does your skirt tremble and sway
But never drop from your hips?
Why do you house your breasts in a blouse
When they freeze for the burn of my lips?

Why do you pray to water that flows
Cold to a colder sea?
I'll burn and I'll dry the tear in your eye,
And coax you to blaze with me.

Where are the tresses that streamed in the air,
Gold as my light is gold,
Why do your feet so tiny and fleet
Sink in the sluggish mold?

Where is the skin, where are the arms?
Where are the little breasts?
The bark of a tree, and a toss of leaves,
And birds in a pair of nests.

Daphne, my lass, you've won the race
And you wear the laurel crown.
Never a man will stretch you flat
And kiss you up and own.

Never a lad will pat your bark
And sigh for the hole in your trunk.
Never your roots will curl in the dark
Where your pretty toes are sunk.

Laurie my bonnie, long may you wear
The wreath of the triumph you've won,
And the birds in the nests that once were your breasts
Rise up for a kiss of the sun.

Dialogue at Dusk

Against the dying day, faint light of nowhere,
I walked into the new light of a street
Forsaken but for random cars that flow where

A little clump of light marks restaurants
Still open, and a measured space of warmth
Invites the seeking and the waiting haunts

Of years in death. And there I sat and waited,
Briefly conferring with the silent servant,
And there I knew that all premeditated

Moments were moving to a brightening vision.
And then I saw him coming through the door,
Certain as God. It was an old decision

That we should meet, and in some vanished place
I made it. Face of all human faces
(Save one) I most desired and feared to face.

In clumsy reverence I rose and beckoned,
Uncertain should I kneel and wait his word.
He turned and smiled, "Perhaps you'll have a second?"

And sat across the little table from me
And smiled again (where had I seen him smile?)
To see the silence that had overcome me,

And spoke at last to tell me, "Speak the lines."
Then in the moment of my loosening lips
The silent servant brought two separate wines.

We chose and drank. Then I to him:
"O thou, implacable and friendly ghost,
Whose laughter, rampant now, now dim,

"But never silenced, is the white consent
Between the blackness of my written lines,
Equally apt to hearten and torment,

"Must thou, behind the closing curtain a third
Of a millennium, consent in silence
And speak no more the revivifying word?

"We are the clumsy pygmies on thy stage
In chronicles of wasted Southern clans,
And social judgments on a stunted age,

"Or else the drunken apes of final night
When glaciers close the chambers of the heart.
Remain, and speak again. There shall be light."

And he: "You know your age; I knew my own,
And knowing it, death had a sweeter savor.
Man does not live, but he can die, alone.

"I lived in the last wraith of that sweet order
Of measured rank from God to lord to clown
To daffodil. I saw beyond its border

"The shape of men to come—the idolaters
Of the black book, raging for regicide,
And next the geometric worshipers

"Of abstract reason, plotting their level roads
With the straightedge through custom's homely hedges
And gentle gardens; building proud abodes,

"Castles of frozen intellect and power,
Where king and peasant once had joked together.
Good Bess could hold them back, but James—the hour

"Was coming, but I won the narrow race,
And left my bones beneath the sanctuary
With a last curse to spare one resting place."

He spoke no more and rose as if to go.
"The plays," I said, not knowing what I said.
He laughed and stayed. "A just and cunning blow,"

He said, and drank. "The general unease
Infected me. I wanted to succeed.
I fled from Stratford and I learned to please

"The rabble of the spectacles. They desired
Blood, bombast, murder, incest, madness, love,
I gave it them, made money, and retired."

"And live forever in the words you gave,"
I answered. "God forbid," he said. "I grant
I almost thought so. I would rant and rave

"In some small part beside the other players—
The smell of rush lights and the actors' grease—
Good friend, remember me when you say your prayers—

"And if in a yellowed book my dramas live
For the curious eyes of those who dig the dead,
Have mercy on me. Close the book. Forgive."

It seemed to me the brightness of the room
Was fading toward a merger with the night
And we were voices sounding in one tomb.

"Forgive me as I trust God has forgiven
For gifts expended in a waste of shame.
I could have been a Sidney if I had striven

"For fairer things—A Surrey or a Wyatt,
Even a Spenser—but I fed my soul
Too long upon a self-created diet

"And it became what it was nourished by.
In New Place through the quiet village night
I sat until the dawn blushed at the sky,

"Trying to fan the flames of youthful skill,
Working to write what once I might have written,
But the words came pouring at their own wild will

"Always in dialogue and scenes and acts.
I stopped. I learned to be a gentleman
And play my role among the village facts."

He paused again and then leaned closer to me,
And said, "Good friend, whatever motion of love
And charity impelled you to pursue me

"And call me briefly back from the dark rest
Beneath the stones of Holy Trinity
Where over me the bread and wine are blessed,

"I thank you for the pity of your heart—
Read, if you must, my story of Lucrece
And Venus and Adonis—there the art

"I might have nourished with a provident care
Put forth some buds not wholly to my shame."
The silent servant stood by an empty chair.

6
SIGHTS

From an Inhabited Planet

This paradise and torture chamber,
This thing alive, this green and red,
This April and December
Of the planets, sped

Screaming and singing
Down the lanes of space,
By gravitation clinging
To the sun's red face—

From Venus comes
No word of water,
From cold Mars hums
No wireless chatter.

The probes of space
Televise back
No smiling face,
No maniac,

No reptile creeping,
No insect hive.
Space is sleeping.
I am alive.

This blue-green ball
Of laughs and groans—
Treat it kindly. It may be all
God owns.

Flight to Detroit

Our spaceship cruised at fifteen thousand feet.
A hundred deaths below, pale scuds of fog
Dimmed and filmed the plain geometry
Of Michigan. Man is the animal
Living by faith in straight lines, certain
That if you have enough of them
One or the other will conduct you somewhere.
From fifteen thousand feet the victory
Of man was manifest—a grid of costly lines
Giving the restless spirit of the race
The choice of north and south or east and west
To nothing definite that I could see.

An older Euclid lay below the newer
For other exploration. Here a stream,
Hairy with trees, writhed in slow curves to keep
A rendezvous with waiting water, vanished
Under white lines of bridge, resumed. There a pond
Or small lake, garlanded with private hair,
Detoured the engineer's efficient thrust,
And kept inviolate, or so it seemed,
A depth, a brightness, and the savage circle
Of the hedge of twisting arms, guarding
A kind of chastity beyond the prison bars
Of the compass lines. But the merging night
Denied what fog had half permitted.
The plane pursued a straightedge to Detroit.
The lights blinked red and green. The vision ended.

A Barn, a School, or a Church

Near Bristol, Vermont

A barn, a school, or a church,
  I am not sure of it yet.
The sides were white as a birch,
  The cupola-spire was set

For a modest thrust at the sky
  Above and back from the door.
We were driving so quickly by
  I had no time for more.

But whether it fed the soul
  Or mind or the winter beasts,
I am sure it was part of a whole
  Community cycle of feasts

And the cupola-spire that rose
  From the barn, the school, or the church
Was anchored in earth, with toes
  As strong as the roots of a birch.

White on White

The snow runs out to the lake.
The lake runs under the snow.
Only the foolish will take
A walk to the end of the snow.

There's white from sky to feet
And somewhere a shoreline bends.
Land and the icescape meet.
One secretly starts, one ends.

The Chaos and Order of Snow

Curry the flurry of snow. Tumbling in chaos
The random flakes skitter and angle, crisscrossing
Paths, as the gusts of wind project and direct them.
Sometimes they nearly skim parallel to dim earth,
But at last, one after one, they settle somewhere—
The pine's tufts of needles, the stiff brown of
blades of grass,
Open patches of frozen earth. It is as though
A great brush, frugally dipped in white paint, had moved
With a motion compounded of wrist, arm, body,
And grazed all surfaces, leaving a dot or streak,
Greater or smaller, here and there, in a pattern
Of white on green and brown, a pattern in the sense
That a pair of dice most often gives a seven.
It comes undeniably as reassurance
When the gusts of wind finally unite and blow
From a steady north, sending the single snowflakes
On a uniform trajectory, rank on rank,
To whiten the world with the semblance of purpose.

The Two Birches

The birch tree on the shore
Bows to the birch in the lake.
Courtesy calls for more;
The ripples weave and shake
To answer bow with bow
And call the stars awake.

I stand at the quiet rim
Where birch tree leans to tree.
Graciously white and slim
A birch tree calls to me,
And moves its rippling arms
To beckon, "Come and see."

But the shore falls fast and steep,
I cannot dive so far.
The princess sleeps so deep
I must go the way of a star
And climb the birch of the shore
To be where her white arms are.

Water Lilies

In the cove, shadowed,
Is a ring, lilies,
That descends, falters,
Rises with waves, ripples,
Or the slight breathing
Of a wind blowing.
In the full center
Is a white blossom.

Darwin without Tears

The brightness faded. Frogs awoke.
In throaty reeds the darkness spoke.

No harmony of perfect spheres
Chimed to my educated ears.

In grunt and squeak and squall and croak
The dark of Darwin stirred and spoke.

Small things ate smaller and the smallest
Invisibly devoured the tallest.

The fittest are the eatingest.
The eaten are the second best.

And I who through the fifty years
Have munched a herd of western steers

And sit here eating and alive
Prove that eaters eat and survive.

Here in My Dry, Square Space

A thousand-murmur tumult is in the leaves
And those that are closest glisten as they sway
In slow arcs up and down from the drenched boughs.

Off the low eaves of this small house the rain
Barely beyond my hand drops in the leisure
Of silver slender columns that break and form.

In the dark woods beyond this dry, square space
Dampness, decay, and the shy, little lives
Rising from old deaths. I almost rise and go.

But I am nearer to the fallen log
Than to the winged maple seed sprouting,
So wall the woodland out and keep me dry;

I'll listen to the meter of the eaves,
And bless the dark things of the dripping forest,
But here in my square space I'll wait and see.

Puddle in the Road

The temporary sea
In the gravel road
Has headlands, bays,
Even an island.
The bombs of rain
Explode in circled circles,
Roll to the farthest shores.
Erosion gnaws
A headland's tip.
A cycle track of river
Silts the basin bottom.
Tonight
It will be a marsh,
Tomorrow a prairie.

Robins in the Spring

Pot-bellied angels of the spring,
They potter on the ground,
Flutter on short flights, sing
A little, hop around.

Their bourgeois vests of mellow rust,
Their wings of decent gray
Inspire an atmosphere of trust.
They are neither Beat nor gay.

Somehow one sees the father bird
Returning home at six
To greet his mate with a loving word
And a drink in his house of sticks.

So he appears to one who looms
Six feet with pounds to match.
No robin points his bill and zooms
At me to play at catch.

I cannot tremble at those eyes,
A reptile's glittering pair,
That scan three hundred sixty degrees
Of edible earth and air.

The timorous worm hauled from his lair
Beneath the soil his armor
Sees lunging allosaurus glare.
I see the jolly charmer.

A Prayer to the Creatures and Their God

River water, float me safely,
Spare the workshop of my lungs,
Rattlesnake in coil of diamond,
Sheathe the sunlight of your fangs.
Thunder crashing, lightning forking,
Aim away your stinging tongues.

God outside this studio,
Take me now and all is finished—
Flame of lightning, bang of thunder,
Flash of fang and water, vanished.
You are God. How do you know
This is your world? I tell you so.

7
VARIETIES

Ropes of Nothing

Christ, do I speak to you because my tongue
Trembles into dried, sterile liturgies
Of bland benevolence with others? Hung
Above the highest pine-thrust of the trees
Along the sensed abyss, hung in fear's crib,
Held by the ropes of nothing, no friend can reach me,
Though I have many friends. Safer the glib
Yes that denies than the eyes that beseech me
Into an answer of the speaking eyes.
But do I speak to you? Words, words, my Lord.
I am not ever short of words. Words die
In noise and idiot fluency. O Word
Of God, who opened mouths of silence, reach
My spastic lips, my eyes. Let there be speech.

Crypto-Jew

My feeble will was helpless to resist.
A special devil took me by the wrist;
He led me to a fence and he said, "Tap."
I gave each post a black mass of a rap.
Before he'd let me sleep he made me finger
Doorknob, lamp, and picture. I would linger
In terror, going down a mental list,
To find what fetish object I had missed,
Until my brother, irascible and kind,
Put the quietus on my ravaged mind
And scooped me kicking, lugged me off to bed,
Where horrors of the undone roiled my head.

Though a firm atheist I bought a cross
As talisman. It was a total loss.
The devils, demons, ghoulies and the things
That go bump in the night grinned in gibbering rings.
We were too poor for Freudian analyst.
I seemed predestined for a lasting tryst
With the asylum at the edge of town
Where from barred windows manic screams slid down.

But happily they called a simple doctor,
The body's honest handyman and proctor,
And he decreed the rite of circumcision.
I lost a tight foreskin, I lost the vision
Of hell. The world came back and smiled benignly,
The deepest natural night caressed me kindly,
And when he took the dressing off, I could boast
A privacy and mind as sound as most.

And that's the way to be a crypto-Jew.
My covenant wound let Elohim's healing through
To exorcise my body, mind and sight.
The grinning ghoulies slouched off beyond the night.

A Christian's nothing but a mutant Jew,
My flesh first learned it, then my spirit knew;
Double of years, I was christened at last
(Another story, another yearstone passed).
Abraham, Isaac, Jacob, if I forget
My Red Sea rescue and great Jerusalem
May I have no heritage in Bethlehem.
Amen.

Homeless Feet

O homeless feet of brother Cain,
I hear you marching in the night.
Steady, the beating of the rain.

A metered anguish throbs my brain,
A conscript rhythm rocks my heart,
O homeless feet of brother Cain.

My pulse keeps measure, pain to pain,
My forehead blazes with your hurt.
Steady, the beating of the rain

Records the Abels I have slain.
How long you pace how long a street,
O homeless feet of brother Cain!

Time is a night, time and again
Left, right, the echo of your feet.
Steady, the beating of the rain.

Against the moment's windowpane
Time raps in rhythm. And I wait.
O homeless feet of brother Cain,
Steady the beating of the rain.

A Sequence of Saviours

Saviour, they say. To save something—gold, time,
face—is not always
A task trusted only to gods. A mere mortal—
Dull, dim, dank—from dawn down to sulk of the sun—
Can boast better, one two three. Today Willy,
Cop at the corner, saved seven, stopped cars cold.

Firemen are paid to save. And the AMA
Of free enterprise is a saviour. Frilled floozies
Save old men from age. Money saves from the law,
From jail. Justice sells dear, buys in cheap market.
Duty can dodder. Gold never shirks. Buy safe.

Jesus, compete, but how? Duty mounts no cross.
Your pay glittered red. In the market brought dearly,
We came high. From hell's halitosis of sin
You rinsed throats that stank, dank, rank. With red lotion
Sweetened our breath. And death . . . Jesus . . . one two three.

Prayer to the Hanged Man

Sever the clever from their cleverness.
Annul the dullness of the flat of wit.
Make beauty neither that nor more nor less.
Destroy (destroy, contain) the rambling hope.
Turn tender faith upon the fiery spit,

And wash the mouth of truth with laundry soap.
Throw love the carcass of a rat to chew,
And hood all goodness for the hangman's rope.
Simplify sex into a common gender.
Eat the green leaves with radioactive dew.

Jack Ketch, thy hands, reliable and tender,
Tie knot, set hood, spring trap, break breath, cut rope.
Take my dark body in a still surrender.
Breathe it. Life, love, my wits, good green, faith, hope.

Silver and Sleep

Silver and sleep. Be it so.
In the count of the starways twinkle a time climb the hill
Still and aglow. Flow with snowing atoms.
Even and pure flute of sight.
Sound. I am found. Cradle rock. There where the light
From the secret center bright in the night pulses slow
Blood of my soul pulse in measure.

Going, Growing, God

Singing softly in the dry dark
Of nightland birds or crickets and the
Boom boom of frogs. I thought. I sought
For a reply. Going, growing.

Returner, stand staring in the
Night that rages ages, boom boom,
And for the length and strength of Jesus
God, creditor and debtor. God.

The Dance in Time

Though nothing's well
All shall be well.

Though all is well
The souls in hell

Scream with five senses.
Jesus dances.

He dances in time.
All is well.

Two Prayers for 11:00 A. M. Sunday

1

Jesus Christ, Son of God,
Come and leap where we sleep here.
Slap us awake.

Jesus Christ, Mary's Son,
Come and lurk where we work here.
Topple the tables.

Jesus Christ, Son of Annas,
Come and play where we pray here.
Laugh us to heaven.

2

Gay Galilean, pain to prigs,
Tumble and bumble me, reduce me,
Seduce: loose me, love me from goodness
Into a jest of joy. Come Jesus.

Letter of Bartolomeo Vanzetti to His Sister, Luigia

(Freely translated and versified from *Non Piangete la mia Morte: Lettere ai Familiari,* pp. 48-51)

Meriden, Conn.
12 January 1911

Dear Sister,

I'm sad to hear that you're not feeling well.
Do watch your health. And if you have problems, tell
Them to your aunts, Francesca especially—
She is a second Mama to you and me.
In the uncertainties of inexperience and youth
You need a confidant. Tell them the truth
Without false shame, listen to what they say.
If you trust in them, you'll never go astray.

You are my sister, I'm your loving brother.
We ought to share our hearts with one another.
If ever there is anything that I can do
Please let me know. I'm always thinking of you.

And now I'll talk of America a bit—
I could tell my tales and make a book of it—
But this time I'll be brief. When I arrived
There was a great depression. I survived—
I was lucky—got work in a hotel—
For ten months drew my pay—everything went well—
Then quit because my temperament didn't fit.
When injustice reigns, I won't be a part of it.
I left New York, came to the country. Here
I've farmed, felled trees, laid bricks. Later in the year
I worked in a candy store. Now I install
Telephones. Saved some money. Spent it all

During the winter. When it's very cold
Outdoor work comes to a standstill. I'm told
There's a good job I can get—a Piedmontese,
A friend of mine, nice fellow, anxious to please,
Is working on it. Here in the countryside
I've recovered my health and strength and pride.
I talk of countryside, but it's a city
Of thirty thousand souls. The outskirts are pretty—
With many little parks and ringed by small lakes
Alive with birds when Spring at last awakes—
There is a public library, high school, grammar;
The streets are noisy with a babel of clamor,
Every language spoken under God's sun.
These alien people like to tease and make fun
Of me. If my English were a tenth as good
As my Italian, I'd rub their snouts in the mud.

Here justice rests on force and brutality.
Woe to the stranger (the Wop particularly)
Who stands up for his rights. The nightstick, jail,
The lawbook are thrown at him. It's a fairy tale,
This talk about the glorious land of the free.
This is a land without civility.
Deprive them of their dollars and fancy looks,
They're semibarbarians, fanatics, and plain crooks.
Just get the bucks and the world is on your platter.
Robbery, theft, or graft, it doesn't matter.
So many make their pile by selling out
Their human dignity; they go about
Spying upon their fellow countrymen,
Jailors hired by the bosses. And again
So many are the blind tools of the priests—
Dragging morality down lower than the beasts.
It's true, religious freedom is the rule—

A new sect can be started by any fool—
No nation has so many religious cults
And such crazy ones. But the results—
You've guessed it—the Jesuits run the show.
The holy faiths of Europe cast a feeble glow
Over here—conscience and wisdom—well, I go
My own way in this modern Babylon.
No cop has laid his criminal fingers on
My throat. In general I get along
With everyone. My soul and health are strong.
I'll never say black is white. If anyone
Dislikes me it's because he's felt my scorn.

You know there's a swarm of young Italian punks,
South Italy types, loafers, whorers, and drunks,
In high price clothes, cavorting night and day,
The Black Hand boys, living on its criminal pay.
I leave them alone. I only associate
With the honest and the literate.

I've gone to English School two years, understand
Almost everything. On the other hand,
I'm tongue-tied when I try to answer back.
I trust myself to stay on the right track,
I trust my strength and honesty and will,
I trust myself and I shall conquer still.

And now my love to all. And do be nice
To Papa. Practice virtue, flee from vice.
Be a good daughter and sister. Blessings will rain
Upon your lovely head, and you will gain
The peace of conscience that the good possess,
And give your adoring brother happiness.

Bartolomeo V.

Poverty

A gloss on Luke 6:20-21

The poor are blessed, poverty is not.
It is a nostril sealed with chronic snot.
It is teeth eaten to the gums with rot.

It is the shoddy suit, the hand-me-down,
The vague unease in better parts of town,
The pretty girls that flinch by with a frown.

It is the social worker's clipboard eyes,
The tenement house of urine-seasoned sties,
The charity ward in which the poor man dies.

Poverty, hugged for Christ's sake by the rich,
Is the Lady that made St. Francis itch.
The poor man smells her armpits, that old bitch.

Uneconomic Determinism

My mother never owned a house,
But still she planted peonies.
Along the public roads
I set out private trees.

From house to house we yearly moved
When landlords sold us out from under.
So Adam Smith would say our spade
Was an economic blunder.

We planted and we reaped
No private blossoms or shade.
No wonder we were always poor;
The grocer's bill, unpaid.

We subsidized the public sector
Without a care for *mine* and *thine*.
I stole my neighbor's apples
Wherever I saw them shine.

We lived in that prehistory
That Karl Marx postulated.
Mine was the world's, the world's was mine,
And we survived, unjailed, unsated.

I cheered for Herbert Hoover
From capitalism's attic.
I own two houses now
And vote straight Democratic.

Port Authority Terminal, 9:00 A.M. Monday

From buses beached like an invasion fleet
They fill the waiting room with striding feet.

Their faces, white, and void of hate or pity,
Move on tall bodies toward the conquered city.

Among the lesser breeds of black and brown
They board their taxis with an absent frown,

Each to his concrete citadel,
To rule the city and to buy and sell.

At five o'clock they ride the buses back,
Leaving their Irish to guard the brown and black.

At six a drink, at seven dinner's served.
At ten or twelve, depressed, undressed, unnerved,

They mount their wives, dismount, they doze and drea
Apocalyptic Negroes in a stream

Of moving torches, marching from the slums,
Beating a band of garbage pails for drums,

Marching, with school-age children in their arms,
Advancing on the suburbs and the farms,

To integrate the schools and burn the houses. . . .
The normal morning comes, the clock arouses

Junior and senior executive alike.
Back on the bus, and down the usual pike.

From buses beached like an invasion fleet
They fill the waiting room with striding feet.

Circuit Poet

Holy Thomas, saint of the Celtic Satan, pray
for us poets now and in the hour before and
after the public reading.

Two jiggers multiplied by the number
Of the weeks he'd been out on the road
Totted and toddied up to a normal load
Of eight, begetting lust instead of slumber.

He read his verse with but a hint of slur.
He smiled, a knowing smile, almost an Elvis.
His eyes zeroed from bosom down to pelvis.
Some of the coeds stirred, audibly purred.

After the reading and another eight,
His cotton-pickin' fingers twitched with hope,
His darting eye was like a telescope
Scanning the social heavens for a mate.

And in the morning, only mildly hung,
And with his honorarium mailed home,
The Visigoth took flight for the next Rome,
Mentally tuning each well-tempered tongue.

Fall in Finland

Furled and fractured. Where the Finnish summer
Fades into a vagueness of yellow leaves, seen dimly
Through softly slanting rain. And the sun's arc
Shortens an inch a day. And the small bird
More boldly comes for crumbs at the feeder.
They say this land is the gift of the ocean,
Vague islands arising from shallow seas,
Linking together, trapped water held as lakes.
Sea and lake, land and ocean and sky
Still marry and merge and confuse. I am not sure
Where is the comfort of definite boundaries.
To walk abroad is a kind of swimming.
They say there is no certainty until
The faintest days and the first white of the crisp snow.

Finnish Saturday

They get up late, but the winter sun, later.
We stand in the tentative gray of a new morning,
A long line of infrequent voices, now
Queuing like vague, uncertain spirits
To buy the libations that affirm and redeem.

Beside us, the liquor store, aseptic
And legal, and locked till ten.
Through the glass we can see the motherly
Cashiers tidying their neat gray hair
And the depraved young men poised by racks of bottles.

Through the opening door we slink in good order,
Like gnomes arisen from cracks in the sidewalk,
Each Saturday face guilty with hope.
Kaksi, they say, and the clerk obeys,
Two colorless bottles reserved in a briefcase.

I shall meet them again when the faint sun fails
And the gentle drunks silently zigzag
From storefront to curb and back again,
Or topple from bicycles that spin a while
And then lie in silence with the sprawling master.

From the doors of small flats where workers exist
The smell of potatoes and fish expands,
And the patient wives reclaim their fallen,
Knowing that Saturday is one in seven,
And a Sunday asleep inters the dead week.

November Night in Finland

The Finno-Ugrian mist
Forbids the alien eyes of moon or sputnik
And on the lakes the teeth of ice bite for the center.

Near and moonfar, in Kalevalan incantation
The little towns of East
Karelia doze through the night of the Slavic bark.

Somewhere on Mars or Venus drowse the Samoyedes
And dream agglutination.
The beating heart of Mannerheim has ceased,

And silent are Sibelius' living hands
Beneath the earth he made an orchestrated rune.
Beside the railroad station

The birchtree glistens white
Its autumn gold ground-scattered like the sands
Of faery beaches asking for the seed of speech.

The Magyars do not sleep.
Kadar has murdered sleep. Or in that night
Say better that his murdered manhood countermands

The natural design of love and sleep and waking
And in its grief requires
A keening at the bedside of the light.

Across the little sea is Tallinn and its towers,
        On bright days rising clear
    As the enchanted city of a drowned

    Remembrance. Viipuri is dark and cold
And alien boots ring out the devastated hours
        From lonely, cobbled streets.

        The softly sifting snow
    Comes now with tender touch to have and hold
The forests of the north. And the forgetful flowers

        Of summer dead and done
    Take deeper rest beneath the secret roof
Of birch leaves speechless in a level trove of gold.

Finland in Winter

The market square in Turku

There is some wisdom here if I could find it—
This market square at four o'clock, the gloaming
Almost a name for night, the final women
Loading the carts with failure for their homing,
The even quietude of Finnish voices,
The blackened forms folded into December,
The corner stand with fiery ranks of flowers—
Three for my hostess, good that I remember—

The wisdom is not here for casual asking,
That much I know, and wisdom of a kind.
The answer is as slow as Finnish granite,
As vocal to the feet as to the mind.
And by the frozen lakes the smoke of saunas
Confers another darkness on the land.
Perhaps, not surely, there I understand.

Nuhjala

It seemed the right bend in the dark road. "Nuhjala?"
I said to the driver; he slowed to a stop.
We clumsily tumbled from the bus, surveyed
By the passive and neutral eyes of the Finns.
To the left, a thin lane; we hoped for the best.
Crossing the highway, we stood at the lane's mouth
In the dark night of Finland asleep
And empty. The sleigh was not there. Always before
It had been day, a horse and sleigh,
        the old servant and the dog.

The bus hovered like a ship reluctant to leave
Ignorant missionaries on an unmapped island.
A flashlight cut the night. The driver crossed,
Took my arm, pointed up the lane. "Nuhjala,"
He said, almost as I had said it. "Kiitos,"
I said, remembering my phrase book. "Näkemiin,"
He replied; the word hovered like a blessing
Or Eliot's shantih shantih shantih. The bus left.
We started up the lane, and after fifty dark yards
The fast complin of sleigh bells came racing to meet us.

It is always that way in Finland. Nothing
Happens as planned, but all ends always well.
If by some transmigration of soul I become
A Martian astronaut, and have to set my spaceship
Down somewhere, ignorant of geography and speech,
I hope I choose Finland. The people will accept
My tentacles and extra ears as my own business; by evening
I will have alcohol to drink and food to eat,
And a sauna for body and soul; perhaps an old man
Will play the kantele; and there will be
A warm fire and a bed for the night.

Next morning we awoke. The porcelain stove
Still radiated its mild benediction in one corner
Of our attic bedroom. From the window
The double line of bewitched trees
Lifted prismatic arms of embroidered ice
Up to the rising sun, on to the frozen sea of crystal.

Country Churchyard in Finland

The twelve hundreds, the church here,
Stones roughly mortared, steep gable,
And the tower standing apart
To ring weddings or the deeper mating with earth.

The trained shovel would discover
Likely as not a bone richness
In the churchyard old as the church,
The white fingers in the dark still groping for church.

By faith know them, for the eldest
Words on the stones, the carved Swedish
Of the old orthography, praise
No names fainter than a grandfather's remembered faces.

Among birches and the spruces,
Trace now the mounds of faith. Surely
They were certain God is the best
To reach hands to, but they knew that God is the Ghost

Who fills space and for this reason
Offers the hands of hope nothing
For the clutch of modest despair
To hug. Sailors that are drifting belly on sea

Will swim desperate in last strength
Straight to some flotsam sea-lifted.
In the last of wrecks any church
Offers fingers something rough to clutch. This is much
To say thanks for when a God flows smooth past your thumb.

A Birthday Letter

Dear Eva,

This has been an autumn full
Of lingering. Indeed it seemed to me
A sort of dry nirvana took possession
Before the leaves were fully turned. Each morning
I walked across the campus, and the trees
Were yesterday. Only the grass consented
To change, as the dun needles of the drought
Were duller daily.

Sometimes, on looking up,
I thought I saw a little more of sky,
But the warm days were steady refutation.
Amid the old gold of the constant trees
Time was stabilized. I kept the ceasefire.

One day I looked at trees more sculptural
Than painted. But the Indian summer lingered,
And time, though operative, is invisible
Still as I part a lake of leaves to meet you.

I know, as children know geometry,
That every leaf will fall, that trees will trade them
To take the graver weight of snow, and soon.
My mind consents to keep the common faith
And say that it must be. And yet I swear
If you would lift your hands and smile and speak
A blessing, the trees would answer with obedience
And bend forever in their golden love.

Kalpa

Here in the thirteen billionth yeaı
Of the current kalpa,
One third expanded,
Exploding toward the speed of light,
To be scattered in a wider loneliness
Before the hestitant reversal,
The gathering momentum of
The gathering-in
Down the straight lines of curved space,
Home to the night of Brahma;

While Vishnu still sustains the aphid on the leaf,
The pretty stars,
You and me,
Let us play local games
And make believe a steady state
Forever renewed.

And when our play is ended
We'll sleep as best we can
Till Brahma's noon

Falters farthest into a sunset
And his twilight is night
When Shiva's flailing arms dance a backward creation.
Stir softly then and hope.

And I will hope beside you
For Shiva's forty-one billion years
And our atoms blaze with all atoms
Back into Brahma's womb's furnace,
Purged of past and love's memories,
Cleansed of all names,
Are sent forth, fire on fire,
To breed and people new worlds.
Amoeba, fish, reptile, mammal, anthropoid,
Thirteen billion years, give or take.

I'll see your smile
And home in.

I think I've loved you before.

Dream

The high green hill
Rose in a soar of hope
To a far sky.
My feet were deep in grass.
I felt the ages pass.
It was very still.
Perhaps one time I heard
A singing bird,
Perhaps a cricket gave a little cry,
And that is why
I failed so long to see you
Standing there
Half a world between my feet and the sky
Hidden to the knees in waves of bright grass.
When I started running,
Songs sang the air,
I took your hand.
We raced upward in grass to the end
Of green and land.
We continued
Laughing and running.

The Angle of the Sunlight

The angle of the sunlight from the sill
Has touched your eyes, the eyes that my lips closed,
And opened them. They close again. The chill
Of early morning has proposed. We dozed,
I think, your arm across me and my head
Between your shoulder and a breast. The rise
And fall of your living lungs was a dreamed bed
Of steady waves floating me face to the skies
Of Christian paradise and pagan stars.
Perhaps we never truly fell asleep
The whole night, while the platinum bars
Of moonlight delved your face pale-high, dark-deep.
The angle of the sun is strong and steep.
I'll kiss your eyes and teach them back to sleep.

Special Relativity

Roll in the darkness, roll the darkness back.
The steel of fingers on your flinty back
Scratches some sparks of anti-entropy
To heat the random slope of you and me.

Last night I almost thought we'd turned the trick,
Given the clock a counter-clockwise tick;
Each pant we were a sixmonth more alive
Until we sighed forever at thirty-five.

I'll get me to the anthropologists,
Clutching research grants in my fist,
Buy them to find a fetish charm
To guard the raven's hair from silver's harm.

I'll grow a soul and deed it to the Devil
If he will tilt the downward road to level.
I'll travel to the speed of light,
And age one second in an eon's flight.

You come along with me and be
(Beyond the parish fields of Mars,
Amid the power of the quasar stars)
My special relativity.

The Halo

Holy, holy, holy. We always knew it,
But dared not say it, fearing
Each the mischief in the other's eyes.

Glenn and Titov know it. They rose, they saw it,
The halo, blue and orange,
Hugging Tellus in a holiness.

Love by faith, my Eva. Though eyes may falter
And only simple senses
Deign to see us as we are, though touch

Delegates for seeing, it sees precisely.
We always knew. Now Titov
Says it, Glenn replies. The glory burns

In a holy girdle. The blessèd planet
Is lapped in God, and holy
We when we renew God's aureole.

The End of Nature

You are my artifact and I am yours.
I made you. I was made. The silly genes
And all societal conditionings
Gave us at most two oblong lengths of marble
For love to cut and purify to form.

Stone learned to bleed and laugh at sight of blood.
Stone learned to generate its pair of wings.
Stone learned to touch and set a sea in billows.
Stone learned to talk, with words and loss of words.
Stone heard the ticking of a mortal heart.

The sculptor's chisel coaxes stone to sing.
The end of nature is the fact of art.

NOTES ON THE POEMS

I wish to thank the trustees of Yaddo for inviting me to spend a considerable period there in the spring of 1966. More than a third of the poems in the present book were completed in rough draft during that stay.

1 *ODES*

Ode on the University of Mississippi. Based to some extent on conversations with faculty members and students who had observed the riot. The main written source is the excellent study by Russell H. Barrett, *Integration at Ole Miss* (Quadrangle Books, Chicago, 1965). The italicized chants are largely taken verbatim or paraphrased from this book.

2 *ELEGIES*

Elegy for a Young Civil Rights Worker. The protagonist is partly a composite, partly imaginary, not to be identified with any particular person or event.

Elegy for President Kennedy. The laments in part two are quoted or paraphrased from various sources. The line, "O weep for Adonais, he is dead" comes, of course, from Shelley's poem in memory of Keats. Tammuz: Ezekiel 8:14 and Jessie L. Weston, *From Ritual to Romance*. Osiris: Henri Frankfort, *Ancient Egyptian Religion*. The section beginning "The tamarisk in the garden has drunk no water" originally referred to Tammuz, and is taken from James George Frazer, *The Golden Bough*.

3 *QUINTINAS*

This is a name I have given, at the suggestion of a friend, to the verse form illustrated by the poems of this section. **A Quintina of Crosses** was the first one I created; the others represent variations and modifications of the pattern.

4 *CIRCULAR SONNETS*

This is a verse form I accidentally evolved while writing **Vermont Road.** Some of the other poems in this section illustrate possible variations. I hit on the name "circular sonnet" because the effect seems to be that of a sonnet veering back to its starting point. Put another way, I find the circular sonnet a cross between a conventional sonnet and a villanelle.

7 *VARIETIES*

Letter of Bartolomeo Vanzetti to His Sister, Luigia. The book on which this poem is based, *Non Piangete la mia Morte* (Editori Riuniti), was published in 1962, while I was a Fulbright lecturer at the Univer sity of Rome; I came on it by a fortunate chance. It is - collection of genuinely personal and private letters from Vanzetti to his family. So far as I know, no English edition is available, nor do any of the recent books on the Sacco-Vanzetti case give any indication of acquaintance with the book. It is extremely valuable for the light it throws on a personality much more complex than commonly believed.

Circuit Poet. A composite but not wholly imaginary figure.

November Night in Finland. The Finno-Ugric languages are spoken by the Finns (including those living in East Karelia under Soviet rule), the Hungarians, the Estonians (whose capital is Tallinn), and various small groups such as the Samoyedes. Viipuri was formerly a city of Finland; now (like Estonia) incorporated into the USSR.

Nuhjala. When my family and I were living in Finland, we often visited at Nuhjala, the country estate of our good friend, Dolly Therman . . . "Kiitos" means thanks; "näkemiin" good-bye.

Kalpa. Based on the current theory of the oscillating, universe, a concept that agrees remarkably well with Hindu cosmology.

Dream. It was.

ACKNOWLEDGMENTS

Grateful acknowledgment is made to the following periodicals, in which many of these poems first appeared:

America: White on White
The Beloit Poetry Journal: The Angle of the Sunlight
The Catholic World: The Spacechild's Reverie; Ropes of Nothing
Charlatan: Water Lilies
The Chicago Tribune Sunday Magazine: From an Inhabited Planet; Dream
The Christian Century: A Sequence of Saviours; Prayer to the Hanged Man
The Christian Science Monitor: Fall in Finland
Dryad: Ode on the First Ape that Became a Man; Ode on the University of Mississippi; Bats at Dusk
Experiment: November Night in Finland
The Ladies' Home Journal: A Barn, a School, or a Church
The Massachusetts Review: Flight to Detroit
The Michigan Quarterly Review: Finnish Saturday (*as* Saturday in Finland)
The New York Times: The Chaos and Order of Show; Finland in Winter; Here in My Dry, Square Space; Puddle in the Road; The Two Birches
Newsletter of the Conference on Christianity and Literature: A Prayer to the Creatures and Their God
Noetics: The End of Nature
The Poetry Bag: Dialogue at Dusk; Circuit Poet
The Reporter: Walking with a Young Grandson; Uneconomic Determinism
Sage: Silver and Sleep
The Saturday Review: Ode on a Plastic Stapes
The Sewanee Review: The Archaic Hours; Homeless Feet
Spirit, a Magazine of Poetry: The Halo; dedicatory poem (*as* The Lilacs of the Law of Love)
Today: The Dance in Time; A Quintina of Crosses
The University Review: Vermont Road; A Birthday Letter; Special Relativity; Elegy for a Young Civil Rights Worker
The Virginia Quarterly Review: Apollo's Song to Daphne; Noah at Ararat